WHAT PEOPLE ARE SAYING ABOUT

CONSCIOUS LIVING MADE EASY

Conscious Living Made Easy addresses the most basic human questions – the ones asked eternally, by every culture in all times: What is life? Why am I here? What happens when I die? Bob Southard, who unexpectedly had to face his own death, explores the issues surrounding this most profound of subjects, delves head-first into those very questions, and then offers experiential methods for probing deep. . .guiding us through a process that is both personal and universal, a way of being fully aware of ourselves, of embracing the aging process, and for planning our transition. Highly recommended!

John Perkins, *New York Times* Best Selling author of *Confessions of An Economic Hit Man, Shapeshifting, The World Is As You Dream It, Hoodwinked* and many other books.

Bob Southard thoughtfully explores how to better live, age and appreciate each moment. Conscious Living Made Easy *is down to earth and practical, with easy-to-apply suggestions and meditations. This valuable guide helps us navigate life's many changes with flexibility and compassion.*

Llyn Roberts is the director of Dream Change, dedicated to the transformation of human consciousness. She is the author of *The Good Remembering, Shamanic Reiki* and *Shapeshifting into Higher Consciousness.*

Conscious Living Made Easy

Conscious Living Made Easy

Robert Y. Southard

BOOKS

Winchester, UK
Washington, USA

First published by O-Books, 2011
O-Books is an imprint of John Hunt Publishing Ltd., Laurel House, Station Approach,
Alresford, Hants, SO24 9JH, UK
office1@o-books.net
www.o-books.com

For distributor details and how to order please visit the 'Ordering' section on our website.

Text copyright: Robert Y. Southard 2010

ISBN: 978 1 84694 516 8

A CIP catalogue record for this book is available from the British Library.

Design: Stuart Davies

Printed in the UK by CPI Antony Rowe
Printed in the USA by Offset Paperback Mfrs, Inc

We operate a distinctive and ethical publishing philosophy in all
areas of our business, from our global network of authors to
production and worldwide distribution.

CONTENTS

Author's Acknowledgements

Providing much needed support in writing this book and throughout my near-death experience are my family – my wife, Michaelene (also for her most helpful and thoughtful comments on this book), my sons Gabe and Matthew and daughters-in-law Sarah and Liz, my sister, Mary Jane, my brother, Dr. John Southard and his wife, Nancy, their sons Rob and Tim, and his wife Carrie.

Thanks also go to my dear friends, John Perkins and Llyn Roberts, who supported me, cared about me and pushed me to look deeply into what my near-death experience was trying to teach me, my colleagues at the Thacher Montessori School for their support, and the staff at the Milton Hospital in Milton, Massachusetts, who made my stay at the hospital as pleasant as possible.

To my mother, who lived in dignity and love and died in dignity and love.

I

Introduction

Conscious living is taking responsibility for what you do, for living a life without regrets, and with planning your life rather than just letting it happen. Everyone's going to die, conscious living offers the opportunity to live the life we want in an aware way.

As children, we think we are immortal. Even as we get older, we think it is "someone else" who will die, not us. We view our death as far off and we have plenty of time to do whatever we want. Conscious living is accepting that death is a part of life and planning for it, while not allowing it to dominate our lives at any age.

Conscious Living Made Easy will guide you to understand and accept death as part of life. The author's brush with death will help you appreciate life and overcome your fear of death. We will explore the reasons why we don't want to die, why we fear it so, and how we can integrate death into our conscious and sub-conscious beliefs (or, as I like to think of it, our spiritual tapestries).

This book will help us open ourselves to the reality of death, while guiding us through the reality of life. It will lead us through some of the key elements for you to live a full and rewarding life.

Not all aspects of our lives will be perceived as happy and wonderful. But, all aspects affect and guide us towards what we need to learn.

We can meditate or journey and have good thoughts and good feelings – when everything is going well. What happens when life isn't as smooth as we would like:

Under a lot of stress at work
Lose your job
Face a phobia
Get cancer or some other traumatic disease
Lose a loved one.

The fact that you're reading this book is a good indication of your desire to live a full life, in good as well as difficult times. However, we are not perfect and can all take steps to improve our attitudes and actions in our lives – at any age. We can choose to have positive thoughts and actions over negative thoughts and actions.

We want to feel and understand the preciousness of life and try to live life to its fullest.

It is never too late to change your life, even if you're 85. You may not win in the Olympics at this age, but you can still fulfill a realistic dream – recognize where you are in life and go from there.

At this point, you're probably thinking/hoping that I'm going to give you some magic words or a meditation that solves all your problems or eliminates all grief.

I wish I could do that, too.

Our responses to challenges of any type are shaped by our experiences in life, the culture we grew up in, our spiritual beliefs, the relationships we've developed and many other factors. I don't believe there is one response for all people to the different situations, problems and illnesses we encounter. We will explore methodologies and firmly establish our core beliefs so that we will have more confidence and internal guidance to help us through difficult times.

A key to conscious living is your spiritual tapestry, a concept I introduced in my earlier book, *Ordinary Secrets: Notes for Your Spiritual Journey.* Briefly, it helps you to face, establish, and integrate your beliefs into your way of being. It helps you to deal with whatever comes your way. You can use meditations, affirmations and other tools which we will discuss to help, and to determine what you like to do and then work towards that. In the background and guiding you is your spiritual tapestry. Certainly, there is no one way that will work with all people. However, I do believe that there is a methodology that we can each follow to lessen the effects of difficult occurrences.

I am writing this book for several reasons. The first is that I truly believe that living consciously provides a much fuller and more interesting life. We should know that our death will happen. And, as part of this process, I will ask you to acknowledge, respect, accept and know that death will come, and can at any time. Instead of fearing death, allow the knowledge of its existence and reality to help you live life more fully – to live consciously.

Another purpose is to discuss some of the attributes of aging so that people of all ages, but especially younger people can more fully understand what happens as they try to deal with this process, and that an understanding of aging will help us as we try to live conscious lives.

Finally, from my own explorations of life, death, spirituality and living consciously, I would like to offer some thoughts and meditations, and offer ways for you to focus your life in such a way that you can identify what you would like to do and develop a plan to do it for yourself and to help others.

You may or may not agree with my views and comments on life and death, and that's okay, but perhaps in reading this book, your thoughts will be stimulated in your own way, deepening your understanding about your own life and death.

Conscious Living Made Easy is experiential. You can just read it, and hopefully get something out of it. However, there are several meditations included which, if used, will help you to understand aging, the fear of death, and determine what you want to do in life among others. I believe that the more time you devote to these meditations, the more you will get out of life.

This book is not about religion. It does involve spirituality, which can be enhanced through religion or not. Depending on your outlook on life, and death, there are different ways to view death:

The spirit or soul goes through a number of lives to learn what we need to.

Whenever we die, that's it, nothing more.

I personally believe in the first, but I'm not pushing one belief over another. In fact, while belief in the first may ease somewhat your thoughts of death, it doesn't, in my mind, change that we should choose to live our lives consciously.

Some, if not many, people reading this book might think, this is okay for you, but my life is different. I'm special, I have more money, I am more intelligent and so forth, so I couldn't or shouldn't adopt your way of thinking about death.

And, to some extent, that's true. We all have different life experiences and have different amounts of money and material goods. Some of us are happy no matter what we have or don't have, what level of celebrity we've achieved, or none at all, but in the end, we all die – the great equalizer.

I hope after you finish this book, you will want to live your life appreciating each other and each day, each tree, plant, rock, the water, and all aspects of the planet we live on in a conscious way that you may not have before. And, do it with love and compassion.

2

At Death's Door

I don't mind dying as long as I don't have to be there.
– Woody Allen

"Have you spent the last twenty years sequestered in a Tibetan monastery studying from morning to night with monks, or hidden away in a cave meditating high on a mountainside in a remote location, living on bread and water? Have you had a near-death experience?

I haven't either."

That was the introduction to my first book, *Ordinary Secrets: Notes for Your Spiritual Journey* in October 2007. Since that time, I still haven't spent twenty years sequestered in a Tibetan monastery, or hidden away in a cave meditating high on a mountainside in a remote location. However, as for the last item, I did have a near-death experience in late 2009. Having used the journeys detailed in *Ordinary Secrets* and integrated the ways of being outlined there into my spiritual tapestry, it allowed me to survive this experience much more smoothly than if I hadn't followed these ways. Perhaps smoothly isn't the right word, because there were some definite bumps and potholes on my road to recovery.

In all truth, though, this experience was still difficult and added a sense of urgency to further process my beliefs and ways of being so that I could live as consciously as possible. I will try to pass on my experience and the lessons I learned to help you enhance your lives as well.

I write about my experience not because I think I am so special (at least, no more special than anyone else), and that no one else has ever gone through what I did, but because I did experience challenges on a relatively limited basis that many thousands, if not millions of people face every day. Every day, people die or contract serious illnesses that change their lives temporarily or permanently. I should be, and am, thankful for what I went through and that I am still living on this plane of existence.

If you have not been hurt or sick or faced a serious medical situation, I hope to impart to you some measure of what the experience feels like so that you can understand it better, to understand that it could happen to you, and to help you understand what your friends or family members may be going through in similar situations.

I had been having cold symptoms for a couple of days, but by Sunday morning was feeling much better, just in time for Christmas vacation. By Sunday night, however, everything changed. I developed a pain on the left side of my chest, at the level of the middle of my bicep. It was a sharp pain that wouldn't stop. I tried lying down, sitting and standing up to no avail. But, it felt as though it was a surface pain so I wasn't terribly concerned.

After about forty-five minutes of feeling this pain, it seemed to me that I should go to the emergency room to find out what was going on. Unfortunately, there was a significant amount of snow on the ground and we couldn't drive out. My wife called our son who has a four wheel drive truck and he came down and picked us up. Why not call the ambulance? I still wasn't taking it too seriously or maybe I was in a state of denial, but we all make the best decisions we can at the time.

I was in the emergency room for about two hours, feeling better and thought I would be going home soon. My wife and son stepped out of the room I was in; I thought to get some water.

That's when it hit. (I found out from my wife much later that she and my son were told to leave, but not why. While they were in the waiting room, she heard a nurse say with a sense of urgency to another nearby nurse that someone had crashed. I guess that was me.)

I was hooked up to a monitor checking my heart beat among other things. I found out later that once it reached around 200 beats per minute, the monitor couldn't accurately track it (normal rate is 60 – 80 beats per minute). What I was aware of is that my body became intolerably hot. My entire body was far hotter than I could imagine was possible. I'm a person that likes to be warm (just ask my family or colleagues at work), but this was immeasurably beyond my comfort level.

At the same time, though there were people in the room and machines beeping, I heard nothing. All was quiet. As I lay there, trying to adjust (for lack of a better word) to this different situation, I became aware that darkness was closing in on me.

I felt then that I was dying, and there was nothing I could do about it. As I considered this, I was surprisingly calm and prepared myself mentally for it. I have no idea how long this took, though I suspect that it was somewhere between thirty seconds and a minute.

I don't know what happened next, or why, but I lived. Some time later, when it seemed clear that the immediate danger had passed, I was moved from the Emergency Room to the Intensive Care Unit. Around ten that morning, my doctor, Dr. Carmel Kelly, said, "God gave you a gift." My emotion was still so raw at that point that I barely managed to squeak out, "Yes." I can't tell you physically why I survived, but spiritually, I know that everything happens for a reason, and I'm still processing that.

I was originally told that I should be able to leave in two to three days. Each day, I was told one more day, then one more, then one more. Ten days after I entered the emergency room of Milton Hospital in Milton, Massachusetts, I finally went home. The suspected virus had affected my heart and kidneys and I knew that correct decisions were made regarding the length of my stay in the hospital. It was still difficult and a bit depressing – much of the depression coming from not knowing when I was going home due to a too slowly changing physical condition or what my physical condition would eventually be.

I won't bore you with the often unpleasant details of what I went through while in the hospital. However there are a few learnings or awakenings that have had a great impact on my increased awareness of what it means to live consciously.

One of the most significant realizations I had, what may seem obvious to many, is that the process of dying or being sick and recovering is a lonely trip. Reflecting on my brush with death, I realized how lonely I felt when I thought my time had come. There could have been a hundred people in the room, and it wouldn't have changed that feeling. This was happening to me and me alone (of course).

As I lay and sat in my hospital room, that feeling, or awakening continued. I would watch television and see people having fun moving freely, carrying on their daily lives while I was enduring needles, restricted movement and pains in various parts of my body. But, it wasn't a 'Poor me,' or 'Why me' kind of feeling. It was a shock, that this kind of thing could happen to someone who for most of his life had been quite healthy, that it could happen to someone who was supposed to live into at least his eighties with a healthy body and mind - that it could happen to *me*.

I'm me, and these things don't happen to me. How many people feel this way, either consciously or sub-consciously? Do you? Take a few moments to think about this.

As I lay in bed and subsequently began moving around – slowly - I tried to figure this out, and one word kept coming back to me – ego. We'll explore more about the ego later.

Even though I finally realized and acknowledged that I would deal with the pain, inconvenience and change in how I lived, myself, I became fully aware of the importance that family, friends, colleagues at the Thacher Montessori School where I worked, and the hospital staff made, throughout my hospital stay and after. My family and friends were always loving, caring and concerned, and the hospital staff, doctors, nurses, technicians, dieticians and cleaning crew always had a pleasant word and expression of concern for me. I had a wonderful spiritual conversation with a member of the cleaning crew. My colleagues at the school were extremely supportive throughout my recovery period. Even though I went through it alone, I wasn't alone.

Once I was transferred to the Intensive Care Unit and then to my room, I found that I needed the room cold (very unlike me), that I needed noise (the television was on twenty-four hours a day), and I needed the lights on twenty-four hours a day to quell the neverending darkness. The noise and light requirement extended for several months beyond my hospital stay. It seemed like a natural reaction to what I had experienced when I thought I was dying, and I think it was. Yet, at the same time, it felt symptomatic of something more.

When confronting difficult challenges, don't shy away from looking them in the face and questioning what their purpose is, and what you are supposed to learn from the experience.

I felt I was handling my near death experience fairly well. Two months after it happened, I was sitting in a restaurant in eastern Massachusetts with a couple of good friends, Llyn Roberts and John Perkins, both successful writers, lecturers, shamanic workshop leaders and healers. We were sitting on deep cushioned sofas and chairs, warmed by a fire in the fireplace and isolated from other patrons by a wall separating us - a great atmosphere for quiet, intimate conversation.

I commented to them what I had said to myself numerous times, "I know I have lessons to learn from my experience."

They didn't let me off the hook with such a clichéd answer.

They backed me into a corner and made me face the reality of the experience I had just been through. They probed, pushed and kept at me to go deeper. As I thought about this conversation later, I wondered, "Were my initial comments just an excuse, an out for dealing with life's problems, or rather, not dealing?" I realized that that was true. That thought and the reality of the experience shook me up and made me think much more deeply about what I had been through, and to do so in a far more timely manner than I otherwise might have done.

This is an example of the importance of friends – they ask the tough questions, no matter how hard they are to face, and for that, I thank them deeply.

I realized later that with whatever else was going on, I was in some kind of state of shock. I was shocked that I could die – before I was ready to. Once I figured that out, that people died every day that weren't planning to, that people faced devastating illnesses that they hadn't planned to, that people lost the use of one or more limbs that they hadn't planned to - every day, I told myself to "Get over it."

While I had accepted that my death was inevitable and was not afraid of it, it took several months to work through it, and I have. Again, the understanding and help of my family, friends and colleagues was critical.

Finally, I'd like to make a few comments about my physical challenges. In the hospital, it was difficult getting in and out of bed – the bed was high, it had railings I had to maneuver around, and my physical strength was lacking. Eating was a chore, I couldn't breathe properly and had to use a device to help get my lungs working as they should, and then I had to start walking around the nurse's station to build up my muscles. When I was out of the hospital, I was weak; doing almost anything just about exhausted me. My heart and kidneys did improve slowly, as did the rest of me. I'm sure anyone that has been sick for an extended period of time, either in or out of the hospital, can relate to this.

All of these challenges did give me some insight into how anyone else going through this, or in many cases, much worse illnesses might feel. Depression can easily set in. In my case, because day after day of having to stay there dragged on, with no indication of when I could leave. This gets extended irrationally to maybe I won't be going home. Then, I do go home, but my recovery period never seems to end. Realistically, I do improve from week to week, but I don't know when I'll be back to my old self, or if I ever will be. Again, it's easy to get depressed.

I realized too, that what I went through pales in comparison to what many people have to live with every day, from cancer to Parkinsons to being confined to a wheelchair for life. My lessons from this part of the experience were very strong. First, get over myself. Yes it was difficult, yes it could have been terminal, but it wasn't. Be thankful for what you have and appreciate everyone and everything around you. More about these important lessons later.

This experience wasn't the end of the fun. Four months later, I contracted Bell's Palsy, for the second time. Bell's Palsy is a damaged cranial nerve that controls the muscles in the face. Typically, one side is affected (though it can be both) and that side droops. Among other things, the eye on that side can't close the way it should and tends to dry out, and it is difficult to eat or drink properly. These two events have given me a clear vision of the frustration, annoyance, despair and ultimately, a further glimpse of the depression that the chronically ill may feel.

On the plus side, Bell's Palsy, in fact, taught me to eat, drink and talk more carefully, or as Thich Nhat Hanh, a Zen monk, would say, I became mindful of eating and drinking. I'll talk more about mindfulness and living in the present later, but this disease forced me to be mindful. I had to be careful and pay attention to every bite of food and especially every drink I took.

If I wasn't, food could end up all over my mouth and whatever I was drinking could easily, at the very least dribble down my cheek or cascade onto my clothes. I found it necessary to talk more slowly and often hesitated when speaking so that I could form the words properly before they babbled out incoherently. As a result, I spoke less (nobody complained about that part).

I was very present with each bite and drink, and appreciated the taste of the food much more than usual. More importantly though, as the symptoms of Bell's Palsy faded and my muscles regained their strength, I had learned to appreciate these simplicities of life in a way that I hadn't before, even after my first experience with Bell's.

Before leaving this chapter about my personal experience with near death, I would like to say a few more words about depression. These are not medical or psychological comments, just some observations of what I've experienced. I imagine many people, especially in illness, have feelings of depression, and I want you to know that you're not alone, and for those who care about you to understand something of what you may be going through in this regard.

I wrote earlier of the discouragement I felt at not knowing when, or irrationally if, I would be leaving the hospital. When I did, there was the issue of the physical weakness I felt, and would I ever get back to the physical condition I was in prior to this virus. My heart and kidneys had been damaged and I was taking many more pills than I ever had before. For a while, the near collision I had with death was also a part of this depression.

I realized too, that it's not just the inconvenience of being weak, sick, or taking pills that lead to depression, but the uncertainty of the future. What helped me through this period was that my family, friends and colleagues were so understanding and supportive, and the staff at Milton Hospital was helpful and very pleasant. Also, my beliefs, my spiritual tapestry, doing meditations, knowing what I was going through was something

I needed to, and looking ahead to the future were a tremendous help. I was fortunate though, in that what I experienced was relatively short-term. This was something more to be thankful for.

You are now, no doubt, on the edge of your seats, waiting for my inspired solution to dealing with difficult and challenging situations such as I've described above.

I must say again that I don't have magic words to do so, however, my experience reminds me to be thankful that I can still enjoy the beauty of life on this plane of existence, to live in the present, and to live in appreciation of, and gratitude for, all the gifts I have been given. Add to this, the attitudinal aspects we will discuss later and we will have a methodology for responding to problematic places we sometimes find ourselves in – not magic, but a way of living our lives to better handle less than welcome situations when they come to us.

We will examine next the changes that occur as we grow older, then some comments on death itself, leading to ways to live consciously and ways that conscious living can help us live a fuller, more rewarding life.

3

Aging Happens

Here be dragons.
– Inscribed on the edge of maps during medieval times –
because they didn't know what dangers might be
lurking there.

Aging is one of the great mysteries in life. We don't know how our bodies, mind or spirituality will change, or how they will affect our jobs, finances, friends and so on. I think former New York Yankees catcher, Yogi Berra, summed it up perfectly when he said, "It's difficult to make predictions, especially about the future."

In this chapter, we will take a glimpse into the future – different for each of us, but the process is similar. Understanding aging is important because in addition to death, it is a constant, not necessarily what the changes will be, but that we will change over time. The way we live consciously, however, doesn't change. We may need to adjust the circumstances of our lives, but the process of conscious living is consistent from one person to the next, and over time.

Do you think about, wonder, or worry what your life will be like as you age, as you move into your seventies or eighties or nineties? Do you think about difficult or debilitating diseases like cancer or heart disease or Alzheimer's? Do you think about death – at any age?

Do you wonder how you will react to any of these or numerous other serious illnesses? Will you grasp for every moment of life that you can get? Will you feel sorry for yourself, or blame God or Allah or Buddha or someone else for any distress that arises?

In my experience and observations of others as they age, most tend to exhibit the same patterns, the same way of interacting with others, and think the same way at an older age as they do at a younger age. If someone tends to be anxious, negative, or unpleasant to others when they are younger, they will likely be the same as they age. Others, who treat people with love, compassion and respect, will also likely do the same as they age. As we discuss components of conscious living further, you will be provided with tools to develop attitudes and goals that may or may not be the same as you have now.

What can you do now? Decide what/how/who you want to be and start working on it now. You can change now if you want to, or later as circumstances dictate.

First, however, let's consider what it means to age – we all will, in some way or other if given the chance.

I thought as I grew older, my taste in music would change to what my father liked, or perhaps as I got older, I would become more like my father instead of staying who I was. I don't know why I felt this way, I just did. As you get older, you are still you – not your parents or anyone else. As you learn and experience life, you can change or not, it's up to you.

As our chronological age increases, we change in some part because we think we're supposed to change. You age, to an extent, the way you think. If you believe that as you get older you will slow down and can't or won't do much, you will probably act just that way. If you see yourself sitting in a rocking chair watching television from age 65 (or when you've determined to retire), then you will. Many people retire at age 65 – fewer today than ten years ago due to economic necessity, but many are able to work far beyond their early expectations. You, in fact, may want to keep working for economic reasons, but also because you enjoy it – you like the work and you like the people you work with. It keeps your mind engaged and can keep you more physically active.

The components of aging include: physical, mental/emotional, and spiritual.

Physical Changes
Some of the physical changes you could experience are:

- Lower energy level
- Can't move as quickly as you're used to and have slower reflexes
- Aren't as agile as you used to be
- More pain and stiffness
- Added weight
- Slower recovery from injuries
- Skin changes
- Eyesight deteriorates
- Hearing deteriorates

Betty White would, of course, scoff at the above. Why is she the exception? Genetics, I suspect is part of it, but attitude is also very important. We'll talk more about attitude later on. But, can you imagine if she decided she was too old to act? What if, at age eighty (at the time of the writing of this book, she is eighty-eight) she decided, 'I'm too old to do this any longer?' She would have given up many productive and fun (for us, too) years.

Mental/Emotional Changes
Some of the mental changes we could experience are:

- Forgetting: names, tasks that we want to do, or have done
- Attitude: can become more belligerent or feel more entitled due to increased age
- Depression: more aware of death and illnesses that occur,

yours and those around you
- Depression: increased awareness of all the physical changes taking place

Spiritual Changes

Potential spiritual changes include:
- Specific beliefs may change: see Chapter 7 for a list of some specific beliefs that may be altered because of aging or your plan for conscious living
- How you view and live your life may change.

The above physical, mental/emotional and spiritual change lists are only partial – add those of your own that you are concerned about and aware of. They also don't apply to everyone – which ones apply to you?

If you recognize and accept that changes will likely take place due to age or illness –and as a result, you may not be able to live in as carefree a way as before. For example, if your blood is thinner than it used to be (and you are taking medication to prevent clots), you will need to avoid cutting or bruising yourself – not that you would want to anyway, but now it will be much harder to stop the bleeding.

It doesn't mean your life comes to an end, that you can't do anything anymore – it is just a change. Now you need to be more careful in what you do, there may be things you can't do any more, and you may need to live differently. You need to evaluate the risk in what you do.

Keep in mind that aging occurs at all ages. When we're younger we don't think of aging, or notice its effects the way we do when we're older, but it's still happening. This book is therefore, also for the young and to help younger people look ahead. It's hard when you're thirty to appreciate the concerns, worries and wisdom of someone in their sixties, seventies, eighties and beyond.

When I was younger, I would look at older people, including my parents, and notice some of the differences between them and me: they couldn't move as quickly or as agilely, and they seemed to have more pains and so on (see the list of physical changes earlier in this chapter).

I could observe these differences but not truly appreciate, understand or feel them. And, at no matter what age I was, maybe until my early fifties, could I imagine that I was becoming what I had earlier observed. Even so, death still seemed remote.

At any age, but especially if you are younger, be observant – watch older people, how they move, talk and so forth. Though we are all different, it is an indication of what to expect and gives impetus to enjoy what you can do today.

Be aware, too, that as you age and change, so does your family, including and especially, your parents. Your relationships between you and your family members most likely will be somewhat the same whether you are ten or forty. Your older or younger brother or sister will still be your older or younger brother or sister no matter what age. The way you feel and interact will probably be surprisingly similar at any age.

The same holds true with your parents. But, your parents are twenty plus years older than you and age – physical and mental - will seem to affect them more and faster than it does you. The relationship that you've felt for most of your life will change at some point. It could be gradual and you notice it as it happens, or you might one day visit your parents and not recognize them as you had a week before. The physical and/or mental changes could be dramatic in a very short time. This could affect your plan for conscious living, unless you have factored it in (though of course you won't know exactly how that will all play out). It also emphasizes the importance of having the financial and other information available that's listed in Chapter 8 on planning.

You should also talk to your parents. What was their life like growing up? What were their aspirations and disappointments? What did they do? Where did they go as their life progressed? What was the economy like? Were there wars? As they got older, what did they think about as they aged – physically, mentally, and spiritually? How did they feel?

Why? It allows you to get to know your parents better, other than just as parents – a big regret for me. For example, my father was in the U. S. Navy in World War I. I wonder what that was like. What was it like for my mother and father in school, and so forth? This knowledge guides you to a way of appreciating your life as you grow older and what to expect – besides, their lives can be just plain interesting.

Also, since your parents provided the environment you grew up in, and in most cases you share the same DNA, it is possible that you could change in similar ways to your parents.

Or, parents take the initiative and talk to your children. Let them know what you were like and what the world was like when you were growing up, what your jobs were, where you lived and anything else that is important to you. Oral tradition used to be a common method of passing along knowledge. It encouraged closeness. There's no reason why that can't be true today.

Keep in mind, that perceptions of growing old and dying aren't necessarily what happens. As part of the discussion about your parent's past (or some other family member/friend), you can ease into questions about how they felt as they grew older and how it differed from what they had thought it might be. I would suggest asking specific questions in a delicate and respectful way.

Example:

What changes have you experienced as you grew older – physical, mental, spiritual, from your twenties to thirties to

forties and beyond?
Were these changes what you expected or different?
These are better than, "Hey, you're old, what's it like?"

The questions can be tailored to fit your experience, interests, and relationship with the person you're talking to. It's hard for a young person to truly know the coping process until they've aged, to fully understand how the muscles change and so on. Talking to your elders can help.

Consider where you are now in life, no matter what age. You don't need to do a full meditation, but just relax and think about whatever changes you have experienced as you grew older – physical, mental, spiritual, from your twenties to thirties to forties and beyond.

Were these changes what you expected or different? Take a few moments to reflect on this.

I believe it's important to take a positive approach to aging, just as it is in every other aspect of life. Recognize where you are in life and go from there. When you get up after sitting down for a while and your muscles are stiff and possibly ache, you can say, "I'm getting old" or you can acknowledge it and say, "It's great to be able to get up and walk."

And, if you keep saying, "I'm getting old," you're convincing yourself – body, mind and spirit – that you are getting old. The more you repeat it, the more you are convincing yourself that it's true. This is not an affirmation that should become part of your life. Or, instead of thinking that you can't run as fast as you used to, perhaps you can run more slowly, or you can walk. These are both okay.

Try it – take a positive approach to life and all its aspects. If we are fortunate, we get to age. Let's use this process of aging as a motivation for living consciously and getting as much out of life as possible.

As we get older and begin to think about retiring, a lot of

people have so focused on work that they have not considered what they might do in retirement. While it's true that people are tending to work more years than before, they also tend to live longer, and whether life continues for one, ten, or twenty years after retirement, early planning can lead to more pleasurable years.

So, even while still working, determine what you like to do and start doing it. If you think, I'll never be a great artist or musician or basket-weaver or historian – so what – do what you do because you like it, not for outside approval. If you end up making some money or being recognized for what you do, that's a bonus. Do it for yourself first. We'll discuss more about this later before we determine our plan for conscious living.

While you can read the words that tell you to change your way of looking at old age (growing older) and what aging is like, to actually change a way of thinking that has sometimes been decades in the making is not easy. It will not happen over night.

Here are some suggestions as to what you might do – add your own:

1. Decide how you'd like to feel, look, what you'd be doing. To help in this – try the meditation below.

2. Once you've determined this – re-orient your thinking to the new way – as if you've already achieved what you want, again using meditations and affirmations.

3. Any time you find yourself thinking the old way – 'I can't do this, I'm old' – let that be a key to remind you of the new way.

4. Find someone in the news who is as old or older than you and who realizes their age in a positive way, and see what they're doing.

5. When someone dies who is a friend or relative, don't think, "That will be me soon." Instead, celebrate their life and their accomplishments. Let it be a reminder for you to live

consciously and get as much out of life as possible.

Meditation for Aging

Sit or lie in a comfortable position.

Take several comfortable breaths, the more the better.

Focus on each in-breath.

Then, focus on each out-breath.

Now, on each in-breath, breathe in positive energy and relaxation.

On each out-breath, allow all tension, stress and negative thoughts to leave your body.

Continue until you are totally relaxed.

After you are relaxed, feel a cool breeze flow through your mind taking away all thoughts and concerns.

Let it keep flowing until your mind is clear.

In this totally relaxed state, feel the emptiness.

For the next few moments to minutes, visualize your life – physical, mental, and spiritual as you would like it to be and evolve in the coming years.

When you are comfortable that you can clearly visualize and feel how you would like to age, fix the image in your mind.

Take a few more comfortable breaths,

And open your eyes.

Here's a shortcut to help you remember:

Breathe

Relax

Clear mind

Visualize aging as you would like it to occur

Breathe.

If you believe, as I do, that thoughts precede actions, this meditation will help orient your mind, body and spirit towards living the kind of life that you would like it to. Factor the results of this meditation into the Meditation to Live Consciously.

I must emphasize two realities:

First, that life does throw us curveballs and sometimes we get challenges (and learnings) that we weren't expecting. Second, the more realistically you visualize your aging path to be, the more likely you are to achieve it. For example, if you set your goal to have the body of a twenty year old at age 105, chances are you will be disappointed.

Let's now look at and acknowledge the end of the aging process – death.

4

Death Is Part of the Journey

To the one who is born, death is certain
For one who has died, birth is certain
Since you cannot avoid either fate
You should not lament.
– From the *Bhagavad Gita*

This book is not about fearing or conquering death, but understanding its place in life, and how to accept and live with it. As the *Bhagavad Gita* has so poetically stated, death will come to all of us. When, or how, in most cases, are the only unknowns.

This is a good time to pause and consider our own mortality. It is a good time to reflect on what we're doing, what we've done, and what we want to do. Just because you reach sixty, seventy, eighty, ninety or more, doesn't mean you should start waiting to die. You don't know how many years you have left, so why not enjoy them.

I think for most of us, even as we watch our parents die, our friends die, people in the news die, rock stars/movie stars die, we don't believe that we will, except in some distant future way. We recognize (and admit) that it's more likely to 'could happen' as we get older – basically impossible when we're younger; it's always somebody else.

Unless a catastrophic disease befalls us early in life, then the likelihood that it 'could happen' starts to filter into our cells, organs and mind as we age.

When someone passes on, there is a hole, a vacuum in your life, even if it's someone you don't know personally, but you know of, or hear about – it's part of life. Ted Kennedy is a good example. I didn't know him personally, and I didn't always agree with his politics, yet when he died, it was almost surreal. He had been in politics and in the news for many years. He was sick and we all knew it, and we also knew that nobody lives forever. But, he was constantly in our lives, and now he's gone.

When a member of the family passes, it is certainly more personal and harder to deal with. And, when we go, other family members will likely feel that way about us.

What can we do when loved ones/friends die, or someone else that we've appreciated?

Recall the enjoyment that knowing, being with, watching, listening to, or whatever our experience with them was like.

Thank them for the part they've played in our lives.

Grieve, miss them, it's part of the process.

I can't overemphasize the value of friends, companionship and a support network at any time in life, but especially after someone close to you has died.

For example, when I first went to the local yarn shop in Duxbury, Massachusetts, several women were sitting around a table knitting and talking. This surprised me. It was not like any other store I had ever been in. I wasn't sure what was more important, the knitting or talking, but after numerous observations, concluded that they both were important. What a great atmosphere for socialization and knitting. This is especially important after a loss in one's life.

I wrote earlier about how lonely dying is, as is being sick in many ways. You are sick, others around you are not. Even if they are, you still must go through the pain and inconvenience by yourself. One of the many messages I received from my near-death experience is to cherish people and the relationships I have now.

Why do we fear death?

Though not a comprehensive list, some of the reasons we fear death include:

- Change, or the fear of change. We get used to life as we currently know it and comfortable with known day-to-day activities and places, and don't want them to change.
- What happens next is unknown. This is a subset of change. We know where we are, but we don't know where we're going. Belief can be very helpful here.
- Loss of family and friends. This is a solo trip we're going on, and we will leave behind our loved ones.
- Concern for those left behind. Will your spouse and children be okay – financially and otherwise?
- Loss of material possessions. You mourn the loss of your car(s), home(s), money, your collection of old baseball cards or whatever else is important to you.
- Unfinished business. Perhaps you haven't accomplished your goals or completed your bucket list.
- You are living a life you enjoy, doing what you want to do, and just don't want to die.

In a very real sense, all of these fears are changes. We have something, then we don't; we know where we are in life, but we don't know where we're going.

It may be obvious by now, that one of the keys to acknowledging that death will occur, accepting it, and minimizing the fear of it, is to understand why you fear it. That knowledge is an important part of the picture that will help us create a plan to live consciously.

You may fear death because of one or more of the above reasons, or perhaps you have others. To help get a clearer picture of your fear(s), try the following meditation.

Fear of Death Meditation

As before, sit or lie in a comfortable position.

Take several comfortable breaths, the more the better.

Focus on each in-breath.

Then, focus on each out-breath.

Now, on each in-breath, breathe in positive energy and relaxation.

On each out-breath, allow all tension, stress and negative thoughts to leave your body.

Continue until you are totally relaxed.

After you are relaxed, feel a cool breeze flow through your mind taking away all thoughts and concerns.

Let it keep flowing until your mind is clear.

Visualize lying in bed at home, or in the hospital, or wherever you prefer.

At this moment, you feel the end is near.

You are very calm and unafraid, knowing this is part of the circle of life.

As you lie there waiting, reflect on your greatest concern(s) about death.

Take as much time as you need.

Now ask yourself why you have these concerns and what you can do about them.

Again, take as much time as you need.

When ready, return to the here and now.

You are still calm and even more relaxed since you have identified your greatest fear(s) about dying.

Take a few more comfortable breaths,

Focusing on the in-breath,

Then the out-breath.

Come back to the here and now.

Open your eyes.

Here's a shortcut to help you remember:

Breathe
Relax
Clear mind
Visualize your death and why you fear it
What can you do about it
Breathe.

I would suggest that you take notes about what you've discovered. You may find that you feel there are more concerns than you were able to identify in your first meditation. Or, you may not have discovered why you felt the way you do or all that can be done to alleviate those concerns. It's perfectly normal – this is a process, and it may take time to resolve, or at least understand all the issues. I think that if you repeat this meditation - with several days in between for your subconscious to work on these matters – you will find that more answers will come to you than you realize is possible.

No matter what your fear, one approach is to look at death as a new beginning, a shapeshift into another form – whether you believe you'll come back or not doesn't really matter – get the most out of your life in the here and now.

I can't say that before my near death experience happened that I was afraid to die, I just didn't want to. At the moment that I felt it was going to happen, I was calm and mostly at peace – because I couldn't do anything about it anyway.

My experience gave me all the drama of dying, illness, depression and restricted living without the permanence of death or long-term incapacity. It helped me write this book with a depth of knowledge and experience I didn't have before (though I didn't consciously ask for this personal knowledge, it's always good to be careful what you ask for when you do).

Now, I look at death differently, and suggest that you not be afraid of death, but be ready for it.

I feel it.

I picture it being me when I hear of another's death.

I have an idea of what others go through when they have a serious illness or physical incapacity.

Ultimately, the more comfortable we are with death, the more comfortable we can be with life. Knowledge, acceptance and understanding of death will better enable us to live conscious, more productive and more enjoyable lives.

In Chapter 8, we'll explore planning for the future and you will be able to factor your greatest fear(s) of dying into your own planning.

We will all die - how we approach it makes all the difference in life.

Now let's take a look at what conscious living is.

5

What Is Conscious Living?

I don't want to close my eyes, I don't want to fall asleep,
I don't want to miss a thing.
– Diane Warren, sung by Aerosmith

Conscious living is about:
　　living in the present moment.
　　living a full, rich, rewarding life.
　　accomplishing goals.
　　treating others with respect, love, compassion, and caring.
　　consciously understanding your beliefs and recognizing and
　　　　integrating the elements of conscious living into your
　　　　spiritual tapestry.
　　synching, blending, or melding mind and body. The mind is
　　　　tuned in to what the body is doing and vice versa. It is
　　　　how to get from where you are to where you want to be.
　　self-awareness and taking responsibility for ourselves.

I have asked questions of myself about my mission in life, what
I am here to learn. These questions for me have been integrated
into my spiritual tapestry and into my plan for conscious living.
I don't think about them separately any longer. I feel a confidence that in living and updating my spiritual tapestry as
necessary and in creating my plan for conscious living, I am
following the path I was meant to. Though I may not be able to
define, analyze or examine elements of my path as we often try
so hard to do, I am comfortable that it is the right way to go.
Ultimately, of course, there is not one correct path for all to
follow. We all have experienced life in our own ways and

respond differently as situations arise. What we, as individuals, need to learn in this life is obviously not the same for everyone.

Part of conscious living is understanding that even if you are living the life you want and are very happy and just don't want to die, it is going to happen, and you need to assimilate this into your spiritual tapestry.

What can you do to help deal with difficult situations?

I could tell you some of the thoughts, concepts and ideas that have helped me. I'm not trying to convert you to my way of thinking about specific ideas, but to suggest a methodology by which you can incorporate your thoughts and beliefs in a way to help you live a conscious, interesting, loving and fulfilling life.

While I can suggest ways to do it, you have to actually do the work. You won't have to go out and run a mile in four minutes (unless you want to), but you will need to do some mental gymnastics to help yourself. You may find that one thought – or thread in your spiritual tapestry – may be enough to get you through the day in a good way. But, it may very well take several. The more you put into this effort, the more you will get out of it.

If, for example, you play tennis and go out and hit the ball ten times to practice a particular stroke, that will help your game somewhat. However, if you hit the ball twenty-five or fifty times, it will help that much more. A professional tennis player will certainly hit the ball many more times, which is why they have reached the level they have.

This is no different – continue to integrate your ideas, thoughts and beliefs into your spiritual tapestry. In Chapter 7, we will do a meditation which focuses on developing the proper attitudes to live the way you want to. Then in Chapter 8, we will do a meditation which integrates what you discovered in the Meditation for Aging into a clarification of what you would like to do and accomplish in your life, and to appreciate it each step of the way. This is applicable whether you are thirty, or one hundred or anywhere in between.

For example, when I think of all the years when I was totally healthy, did what I wanted – play tennis, run five miles, whatever – I kick myself for not fully appreciating what I had. Don't let that opportunity go by. Look at your good fortune every day, no matter what shape it takes, and be thankful.

You can also look around for inspiration. Matt Brown for instance, was a high school hockey player who fell on the ice and became a quadriplegic. He's fighting back, though, and appreciates what he has now - a twitch of a muscle is a major accomplishment. He has a great attitude, and though I'm sure he has his down moments as we all do, he's working hard to regain what he had before. Go Matt!

When you consider the potential physical and other changes that might occur at any point in your life, this should give you additional impetus to enjoy what you can do today.

If you are sick, physically incapacitated or restricted in any way, you might think, 'What advantage does conscious living give me?'

Conscious living is much more a mental/spiritual concept than physical. It has its physical aspect, of course, to try and live as physically fit as possible, but much more than that is to live an aware, appreciative life no matter what your physical circumstances. Conscious living can help you in the acceptance of your physical situation and to help you live with less stress.

Conscious living is about learning how to live, and I would suggest in a positive way, with positive thoughts every day. We all have things to be thankful for.

How to look at life/ how to live

If you've had one heart attack or stroke, there is a certain fear that there could be another one and this will be the big one. But, you don't have to live in fear or allow the fear to control you.

Although there is not one answer for everyone, there are

certain steps everyone can take to live a more conscious life, recognize that death is inevitable, and live a more stress-free life.

In the coming chapters, I will try to present a number of different thoughts, approaches, and steps to living a conscious life, a life lived for life and not in fear of death, but respecting it as part of our overall cycle of learning and growth.

All of the fundamental changes you may make in your life may not be easy. But, I can tell you some things that are easy. When you step outside, notice and appreciate the sun or moon, the clouds, trees, rocks, flowers, plants, grass. If you live in the city, enjoy the sun, the shadows on the concrete, the hum of traffic, and especially the energy of the people. You can easily be conscious of your surroundings, of the life around you, of your family and friends. If nothing else, this awareness adds fullness and depth to your life and makes it far more interesting than walking around in a haze. And, don't just look at it, appreciate it – appreciate that you are alive to see it and be a part of it.

6

How to Live a Conscious Life

Do not go gentle into that good night.
– Dylan Thomas

There is no reason to "…go gentle into that good night." In these next pages, I'm going to offer some thoughts and ideas for integrating conscious living, aging, and the acceptance of death, and in Chapter 8, we will talk about how to create a plan to determine the life you want and select the road to take you there. This will help you to not only enjoy your life, but also assist you in achieving peace of mind.

I mentioned in the last chapter questions that most of us ask at one time or another, "Why am I here? What is my purpose?" I've integrated these questions into my spiritual tapestry and think that most people spend too much time thinking and worrying about them. If we live a life where the base is love, caring and compassion, where we appreciate and are thankful for all that we have, and we do the things that are appealing to us and resonate with us, then we are living the life we came here to live. We are being guided in this way by our higher selves, to learn what we need to learn, often not thinking of this as our path at all.

Instead of trying to figure out who you are, I'm suggesting that you decide who you want to be, and create a plan to make it happen. In our attempt to integrate aging, death, and conscious living, I believe we need to consider two levels of our being. The first is the conscious or action level, which includes living in the present, accepting change, and facing your ego as well as actually doing the tasks that are in your plan to live consciously.

The second is our attitudinal level. This consists of attitudes and beliefs that have become our spiritual tapestry and create the way with which we approach and live our lives and interact with others. This level will be discussed in Chapter 7.

In Chapter 8, we will put these together and develop a plan for living the way we'd like to.

Living in the Present

After my near-death experience, I thought, 'I have to make the most of my life; I have to do.' I soon discovered that it isn't just about doing, it's about being as well.

We can lament about how life today is different than in the past (yes, change does happen), and how we hope that the future will be better, but, we can only actually do and be in the present. What we do in the present will affect our future.

The concept of living in the present is simple: be focused on what you're doing now, not what happened in the past, and not what might happen in the future. There's nothing wrong with looking back to enjoy and learn from what happened then, or thinking of the future, but the 'do' is now.

It seems obvious that we can only do things in the present. Doing is part of our action, but focusing and being aware of what we're doing is another part. Have you ever been driving your car and suddenly become aware that you don't know where you are or even how you got there? And, it happens on a road you drive every day?

You were driving in the present, but your mind was focused on something else and so you don't actually know what you did or how you did it.

There are other instances whereby you not only know what you're doing, but are acutely aware of everything happening around that 'do.' You are truly in the present.

For example, I had many interactions with my children while

they were growing up, some I remember very clearly and some not so much. In one instance, I was working at home, and my oldest son, Gabe, who was two years old, came into the room I was in and sat on my lap eating a cookie. It was a precious moment for me, and while it was happening, I was very present, fully aware of what was happening, and enjoying the closeness of my son while working.

Another such moment came when I was cutting the hair of my youngest son, Matthew. Again, there was a wonderful closeness. Though he wasn't particularly pleased with my cutting his hair, the look on his face was priceless and I enjoyed every moment of the experience.

If I was not in the present during these times, I know that I would not remember these happenings as clearly as I do. In fact, this is likely one of the main reasons we don't remember more events from our past; we weren't fully present for both the 'do' and the awareness when they occurred.

There have been a number of times in my life, though not as many as I'd like, when I have been so aware and conscious of what was happening, that time seemed to slow down. You, too, have no doubt had these moments of conscious awareness. Take a couple of minutes now to remember them. Pick one and examine it. Do you remember how you felt, what you saw, what was said? Do you remember the colors and the smells around you?

By living a conscious life, a life in the present and with other attributes which we'll discuss, we can have more of these moments.

It is important to remember that every day and every moment of every day is special, never to be repeated. We should live each moment as it passes and savor it.

We often feel nostalgia for the "good old simple" days when life was so much easier. Much of that is mis-remembering the past. In the present, all the agonizing detail surrounds us everyday – the good can easily get lost in the pain. In the past, the painful spikes get rounded and smoothed with time, allowing the good to become predominant, which in itself is okay. But, it tends to make us overlook the good in the present in favor of the 'remembered' past.

If you really put yourself back there, you will, in many cases, find it wasn't necessarily simpler, you've just "forgotten" the more difficult aspects of it. And, someday (like tomorrow), today will be the past and we could very likely think of today as the simpler time – or – think, 'aren't we glad we're not going through that any more?'

The future holds our hopes and dreams. You think, 'someday I'm going to…' Fill in the blank with your wishes. We can chart a course for what we'd like to happen in our lives, in our dreams and in our musings throughout the day. But, we can only make plans in the present. Be in the present – use what you've learned over the years now – in the present – to help you carve out a future that's consistent with where you want to go. Not to oversimplify, but you may decide to paint tomorrow. You've made that decision today, in the present. Then, when tomorrow comes, it will then be today and you can begin painting in the present. It's always the present when you do.

Another, perhaps more useful example, is if you know when you go into work tomorrow, you will have many things to do and can't imagine how you will get them all done. Because of this, you begin to worry, which can raise your blood pressure, increase your heart rate, maybe make you sick and you won't be able to sleep at night (I think I've just defined stress).

You can worry all you want, but you can't do anything about it until tomorrow. Why not try this:

- Meditate and relax. Try the Meditation Simple in Chapter 9, or the other meditations listed there, or just sit and take a few breaths. Obviously, this doesn't make your workload go away, but it does put you in a better frame of mind to deal with it.

- Make a plan today for what you can do tomorrow. Prioritize your tasks and resolve to do them in order, one at a time. When I do this, the fog dissipates, confusion ends, and I begin to relax. I know that in reality, there will likely be interruptions, but I can work through those and go back to where I need to because I have a list, a plan, a focus.
- Get some sleep now that you have a plan and wake up refreshed. The next morning, execute your plan in the present.

See the section on planning for much more detail on how the process works to guide your future to happen the way you want.

What is being in the present, or being mindful like? In addition to the above it can manifest in many ways. As I mentioned earlier, after my session with Bell's Palsy, I pay much more attention to my food and how I eat. I pay attention to the water and other liquids I drink and appreciate having them in a way I never did before.

Other examples of being in the present include:

- When you walk, pay attention to each step and the environment around you. Are there trees, flowers, buildings? Is it raining, is the sun shining?
- When you are with someone, do you listen, do you later remember your conversation?
- In between activities, do you focus on your breath? This is not only relaxing, but can minimize thoughts that you might not want to have anyway.
- When I wake up in the morning, I look out the window and feel gratitude that I can wake up, and for the trees and bushes outside my window.

- I've found that being present commuting to work – observing the trees, grass, an occasional stream, and the sky, for example (while also being aware of the traffic around me) makes for a fuller, more complete, less stressful drive. When driving, instead of going into a trance staring at the bumper of the car in front of you, become aware of your surroundings – driving safely and legally at all times, of course.

All of the above are free. You don't have to go out and spend hundreds of dollars to enrich your life.

One of our current buzzwords is 'multitasking,' or doing more than one thing at a time. If there was ever a word to not describe living in the present or mindfulness, this is it. If you're with a friend, talking and sending a text message while drinking a soda or coffee, you are not truly focused on any one of the three. Chances are you may miss some of the conversation with your friend and you certainly won't properly taste or enjoy your coffee. Particularly with all the electronics available, we think we are doing more, but it can be so much less meaningful.

Living in the present is an important part of conscious living. Below is a meditation to help establish in your mind that you do want to spend most of your time in the present. You'll notice that the beginning few lines are the same in each meditation. They are simply there to help you relax and open your mind to the task at hand. Feel free to change this opening section in any way that helps you to relax.

Meditation to Help Live in the Present
Sit or lie in a comfortable position.
Take several comfortable breaths, the more the better.
Focus on each in-breath.
Then, focus on each out-breath.
Now, on each in-breath, breathe in positive energy and

relaxation.

On each out-breath, allow all tension, stress and negative thoughts to leave your body.

Continue until you are totally relaxed.

After you are relaxed, feel a cool breeze flow through your mind taking away all thoughts and concerns.

Let it keep flowing until your mind is clear.

Visualize that you are in an area surrounded by trees, flowers and grass.

There is a gentle rain falling.

You watch the raindrops splash on the leaves of the trees and fall in slow motion to the ground.

Your focus on this microcosm of life is living in the present, being mindful.

You will carry this forward to the rest of your life,

You will remember the past,

Focus on and be fully aware of the present,

And know that your plans for the future will be made in the present.

Add this feeling and knowledge to your spiritual tapestry as a way of living.

Focus on and enjoy the relaxation you feel.

When ready, return to the here and now.

Here's a shortcut to help you remember:

Breathe

Relax

Clear mind

Focus on rain falling

Focus on the present

Breathe.

To sum it up, our lesson from Living in the Present is to learn from and enjoy the past – plan for the future – do in the present.

Accepting Change

Change happens.

How to face and accept change is important, not necessarily what the change is, because not every change that affects your life will be dramatic. Getting married, having a baby, becoming permanently physically challenged, moving and changing jobs are rather dramatic changes. Most day-to-day changes are mundane and hardly noticeable.

Things do change all the time, though. Each change is an event, neither positive nor negative. We assign values – this is good, that is bad. Someone else might look at the same event in just the opposite way. One of the "secrets" of aging and facing eventual death is approaching change in an open, accepting, yet realistic way. Recognize the beneficial effects of change while also acknowledging the challenges that might occur. However, entering into each change in an upbeat way is a good start.

Now, I can hear the skeptics saying, "Easier said than done. I had a job, and today my boss told me I was laid off." This is a major change and has added a great deal of uncertainty and stress to your life. It could very well disrupt your plan for conscious living (the basic principles don't change, but the specifics of how or what you are trying to accomplish may require a new plan). You don't know what life will be like. Not to in any way minimize the enormity of the change, but it is change, and the process for accepting it or most other changes is similar.

This is an example of a situation, an event that is challenging. We have, in most cases, been raised to look at the negative side of life's occurrences. You can't stop change, but how you react to it can make a huge difference in your life. If you can develop an approach to change in which you realize that it will happen, and face it with a positive attitude, it makes life so much easier and is part of and critical to conscious living. If it's change that you like, great. If it's change that you don't like, accept that it's happened and set goals to transform it into something you do like.

I heard Jonathan Katz, a comedian, on the radio recently. He spoke of his Multiple Sclerosis which he had contracted fifteen years ago. He didn't bemoan his fate. He recognized that there was a change in his life and he would need to live with it in the best way possible. He said, simply, "It's the beginning of a new style of life." I can't say it any better than that.

Working with the Ego

Ego plays an important role in all our lives. It has, of course, a valid role, to identify us to ourselves, to identify us physically and mentally, to help us recognize that though we are individual spirits, we are also part of the whole of humanity.

Ego, on its negative side, can make us feel that we are better than the next person. It can account for racism and other potentially discriminatory differences in our bodies and ways of living. If someone's skin color, religion, or sexual orientation is different than mine, my ego can convince me that they are inferior to me. If I have more money and toys than the next person, isn't that proof that I'm better?

These scenarios ignore the fact that we are all human beings and that we are all spiritual beings. Each one of us is, at heart, the same as the next person.

Recently, two people in two days fell through the ice where they had been trying to ice fish. This was after several days of forty degree weather and warnings not to venture out onto the ice.

Why? They probably couldn't imagine that anything would happen to them, that they would be all right – ego.

Why don't we think we will die? It's always someone else. We watch the news and when we hear someone has died, we usually think or say, "That's too bad." But we "know" that it couldn't have happened to us – no matter what the reason -

accident, natural causes or murder. Our ego has convinced us that we are too good and too necessary to die.

While recuperating from my "experience," I'd watch television, see everyone enjoying themselves, or pretending to, and living their lives normally, even though I was hurting, even though I was sick, even though I almost died. How could they do that?

My ego would, from time to time, get in the way of my common sense.

To help maintain the ego in perspective, try the Journey to Ego. This journey/meditation was first offered in my book *Ordinary Secrets: Notes for Your Spiritual Journey*, and I think it bears repeating here.

Journey to Ego

Take several comfortable breaths, focusing only on each breath.

By now, this should trigger your body to relax to a reasonable level.

Imagine you are standing on the shore of a lake.

The sun is shining and the temperature is just the way you like it.

You see the sun reflected in the smooth surface of the water right next to your reflected image.

You feel safe, comfortable, and know that everything is all right.

You want to experience who you are without your ego running interference and putting its layer of self-interest on all that you do.

Watching your reflection in the lake, gently step back and away from your ego for a few moments.

You can now see the sun reflected in the lake, next to your ego and you.

Do you feel any different?

If you haven't already, allow your body to fill with pure love, compassion and harmony.

Enjoy that feeling for a few moments.

Now, maintaining your feelings of love, compassion and harmony, step forward and integrate your ego back into your body.

How do you feel now?

Do you feel your ego in moderation?

Maintain that feeling.

Come back to the here and now.

You likely feel relaxed and have more compassion for others. Hold onto this feeling as you continue on your path, and repeat this exercise whenever you feel your emphasis in life is too much oriented towards yourself.

Here's a shortcut to help you remember:
Breathe
Relax
Clear mind
Visualize yourself overlooking a lake
Your ego steps aside
Breathe.

In my Reiki practice, I have trained myself to set my ego aside using the imagery from above. While still knowing that my ego exists, this meditation moves my ego out of the way and allows the Reiki energy unfettered access through my body. With just a bit of work, you will be able to put your ego in its proper place in your life.

7

Integrating Other Aspects of Conscious Living

Believe nothing, no matter where you read it or who has said it,
not even if I have said it, unless it agrees with your own reason
and your own common sense.
— Buddha

We've talked about some key elements in living a conscious life: living in the present, accepting change, and working productively with the ego. These are the conscious components of our planned achievements in conscious living. How we approach and enact the various steps in our conscious living plan I look at as our attitudinal level. Those attitudinal elements are in fact, a wonderful way to live our plan (our life). Some of the key attitudes are appreciation/gratitude, love/compassion, and living your spirituality.

I feel that these attitudinal components to how we live out our plan can make life more pleasant, for ourselves and those around us, less stressful, more meaningful and more fun. The sum of these components is to live a positive life, to acknowledge, accept and be thankful for what you have, rather than what you perceive you don't have. This lack could be conceived of as money, cars, homes, or all kinds of material and non-material things.

You may feel there are other components and by all means, add them.

In the next chapter, we'll talk about constructing our actual plan: Who do we want to be? Where do we want to go? What do we want to accomplish? Where do we want to live? And other considerations. You will, I'm sure, have other factors that you want to figure into your plan.

Appreciation/Gratitude

The concepts of appreciation and gratitude cover a lot of ground. As I'm using them here, I'm really referring to appreciating everything (to be defined in a moment) in the present. It is certainly valid and appropriate to appreciate what has happened in the past. It is more difficult to appreciate the future since you don't know what it will be.

By appreciating everything, I mean appreciating the moment, appreciating the positives that change can bring, and appreciating how your ego can help you as you define yourself. It goes much further than that, though, to appreciating the day, your family and friends, trees, flowers, water, the earth, the sky, the sun and much more. Appreciate that you can walk, see, hear or whatever gifts you have.

Put the beauty of the day, where you are, who you're with, and what you're doing in the front of your mind. Like many indigenous peoples do, appreciate the food you eat, the water you drink, the earth we live on. Appreciate solitude when you have it.

Add your own here.

By appreciating what is around you, you open yourself up and make yourself aware. Instead of existing mindlessly, you enter a mindful state with your appreciation.

Appreciate and be thankful for every day you've lived – many people haven't made it as far as you have. Resolve to make whatever is left the best you can. Be in the present, appreciate the present. You won't get this day, hour, or minute back. It's never too late to change/appreciate your life.

Gratitude may, at first glance, seem little different from appreciation. Appreciation is acknowledging that there are many things in our lives that are good. Gratitude is expressing thanks for all that we appreciate, for all the good in our lives and for all the lessons we receive.

Gratitude recognizes that there is someone other than you that has provided all we have to appreciate. It is, by its nature humbling and sends a message to our ego that it is not the omniscient force it may think it is.

Love/Compassion

It's easy to love a baby or child – to feel and react to their innocence and unconditional love. Or, love can be as simple and important as holding the hand of someone in the hospital, or sick in bed in a nursing home or at home, showing that you care, establishing a physical connection and offering comfort all at once. It's easy to feel and show compassion to someone who is seriously ill, has lost their job, is homeless or recently lost someone they love.

In a way, I'd like to get all new agey or go back to hippie days and say that we should all love each other and feel compassion for everyone. That's really a good idea, but frankly, not realistic.

I'd like to suggest instead, that rather than look at love and compassion as two separate emotions, that the caring, positive and wonderful feelings both generate be blended into one as they are integrated into your spiritual tapestry. The intent is not that you'd love and feel compassion for everyone you encounter in life (though, what a great way to live), but to create a more gentle you. Instead of feeling hate, for example, this intense emotion could be tempered with the blended love and compassion available in your spiritual tapestry. This feeling would affect everything you do.

Spirituality

We are all on a journey in this life on earth, a spiritual or non-physical as well as physical journey. By spiritual, I am not referring to religion, though religion, any religion, can be a component of this journey, a way to celebrate and honor the spiritual. I've also found for myself, and I believe for any one else, that it is not necessary to alter your previous religious beliefs, although that, along with other changes in what you have known may very well be altered.

I have spoken of a spiritual tapestry. This is an ethereal repository for our spiritual beliefs and other contributing factors of our way of life. It consists of beliefs such as:

A belief in God (or not),

A belief that everything happens for a reason – and, everything we do is part of our plan whether we realize it or not,

We plan our lives before we come physically to earth,

If you believe in the after life, both birth and death are shapeshifts to a different form,

If you believe this is the end, that there is no more, that reincarnation doesn't exist – it's all the more reason to accomplish what you can in a loving, compassionate and appreciative way while you're here – through conscious living.

We are all one - on the spiritual level, we are all part of the Supreme Being (no matter what your name for him or her is), and therefore, part of each other.

And many more – insert your own here.

It can be helpful to make a list of the beliefs and potential beliefs you have. We will do a meditation shortly in which you can examine your current beliefs and potential beliefs to make sure they fit you at this time. Then you will be encouraged to assimilate the appropriate beliefs into your spiritual tapestry.

Other contributing factors to the contents of our spiritual tapestry include a collection of very personal concepts that have gone from conjecture to, at least in our minds, certainty about how we exist in this physical body and what may lie beyond the physical that we know with our senses. Woven through these beliefs is the way we choose to act and interact with others on our conscious level. Our way of life may include appreciation, gratitude, compassion, and love. Again, this is only an example. Your way could include these and others in any kind of mixture.

Be comfortable with your beliefs to the point where you live your life according to them, without necessarily remembering each one on a daily basis.

Meditation to Determine Beliefs

Sit or lie in a comfortable position.

Take several comfortable breaths, the more the better.

Focus on each in-breath.

Then, focus on each out-breath.

Now, on each in-breath, breathe in positive energy and relaxation.

On each out-breath, allow all tension, stress and negative thoughts to leave your body.

Continue until you are totally relaxed.

After you are relaxed, feel a cool breeze flow through your mind taking away all thoughts and concerns.

Let it keep flowing until your mind is clear.

Visualize that you are on a beach.

The waves are gentle, providing a soothing sound.

The temperature is just right.

You are wrapped in a comfortable blanket of fog, and feel as though you are floating in a gentle breeze.

Open your spiritual tapestry as though it were a book.

You may not initially realize it is there, but it is.

Read it – what beliefs do you find there.

Are these the beliefs you are comfortable with?

Take a few moments to consider each one.

If you find a belief that does not comfortably resonate with you, erase it from your tapestry.

Are there other beliefs you would like to add?

If there are, do so now.

See them written on a page in your book.

Feel them integrate into your spiritual tapestry.

Relax.

Focus and enjoy all that you feel.

When ready, return to the here and now.

Here's a shortcut to help you remember:

Breathe

Relax

Clear mind

What are your beliefs

Integrate them into your spiritual tapestry

Breathe.

I would suggest here that you either tape or have a friend read this meditation to you so that you can truly relax into it and receive its full benefit. It should also be repeated periodically to continue examining and reinforcing your beliefs. There will always be challenges, that's part of growing and learning – at any age. But, how you approach the challenges makes all the difference. If you live your life with a background of peace, happiness and calmness, any challenges will be handled much more easily.

We've identified our beliefs above and have at least begun the process of integrating them into our spiritual tapestry. A meditation follows that guides us in ways of living our beliefs and in living a conscious life. It encourages us to live a life of love, compassion, appreciation and gratitude.

Meditation to Develop Proper Attitude

As before, sit or lie in a comfortable position.

Take several comfortable breaths, the more the better.

Focus on each in-breath.

Then, focus on each out-breath.

Now, on each in-breath, breathe in positive energy and relaxation.

On each out-breath, allow all tension, stress and negative thoughts to leave your body.

Continue until you are totally relaxed.

After you are relaxed, feel a cool breeze flow through your mind taking away all thoughts and concerns.

Let it keep flowing until your mind is clear.

You know that your beliefs and the way you choose to live your life will affect your plan for conscious living.

You may choose to live your life by replacing anger with love,

By replacing hate with love,

By replacing judgment with love and compassion,

By appreciating all things and feeling gratitude for all aspects of your life.

Add any other ways of being that feel comfortable for you and fit your life the way you want it to be.

Take as much time as you need to absorb all of these wonderful thoughts and feelings into your spiritual tapestry.

When ready, return to the here and now.

Take a few more comfortable breaths,

Focusing on the in-breath,

Then the out-breath.

Open your eyes.

Here's a shortcut to help you remember:

Breathe

Relax
Clear mind
Visualize replacing negative emotions with positive ones
Feel appreciation and gratitude for your life
Come back to the here and now.

Again, I would suggest that you either tape or have a friend read this meditation to you so that you can truly relax into it and receive its full benefit. This is an important meditation and I would suggest that you repeat it at least every other day for a month. Repetition will implant this way of being firmly in your conscious and sub-conscious levels. Because everyone is different, it may happen sooner or it may take longer. What is important here is to make it a part of you.

Perhaps the easiest way to sum up what we've covered in this chapter and a shortcut to remembering positive aspects of the attitudinal side of conscious living is: "Do unto others as you would have them do unto you." The Golden Rule. In other words, treat others the way you would like to be treated. Or, for something novel, treat them better – with respect, love, compassion, caring, and with no thought of reward. Be pure in your kindness.

8

Planning Your Conscious Life

If you don't know where you're going,
any road will take you there.
– George Harrison, *Any Road*

Before we go into the details of the planning process, there are some further aspects of this plan that I would ask you to keep in mind.

Be aware that the plan may need to change due to a number of influences. You may find that your personal interests have changed. Something you were doing or thought about sparked an unknown interest that you want to pursue. An illness could dramatically change your life. Or, illness or death of your spouse, parents, other family member or friend could alter the direction you want to take.

It's important to keep this in mind, so that when 'change' does occur, you'll be able to make adjustments.

Planning for conscious living consists of two aspects of your life. One is to plan, at any age for what you want to be and do. The other part of the plan, at any age, is to look outside yourself, to plan with others in mind. This consists of helping those who would be left after your death or in the case of serious illness – at any age.

I keep using 'any age' to emphasize that whether you are thirty or eighty, planning is appropriate, and you can be very helpful to others by providing some basic, but useful information to those left behind. I'd like to talk about this first because defining these key items provides a clearer, more unfettered path for you to live your life consciously and with less concern.

Planning With Others in Mind

There are a number of areas outside yourself to consider as you plot your life to come. They will of course vary depending on each person's circumstances, but some items more geared to help others in the event that something happens to you include:

Financial

What are your family's financial needs upon your death or serious illness?

Do you have a will? This is a good idea anyway, but especially if you are divorced, this is a necessity.

Is there a list of bank accounts, investments or other financial vehicles, including an account number, location, phone number, address and contact for each account (if any)?

Is there a safety deposit box at a bank, safe or fireproof box at home – where are they and where is the key or what is the combination?

What are the usernames and passwords for any pertinent internet sites, including Facebook, or other social media sites, or, and especially, any investment/banking accounts?

Who is your lawyer (if any), including phone number and address?

Do you handle the checkbook and all finances? If so, does your spouse know what to do?

Health

Have you prepared a Health Care Proxy so that someone can make critical healthcare decisions for you? Have you written down your preferences?

Is a nursing home/assisted living a good option – especially important as we get older.

Living arrangements

Do you want to live alone?

Can you take care of the house and yard?

Do you have children that can help?

Moving can be difficult emotionally as well as physically. This too, is change.

Have you examined and resolved the potential issues around this kind of change?

Funeral arrangements

What kind of service would you like and who should conduct it?

Where would you prefer to be buried?

Do you want to be cremated or not?

Who should be pallbearers?

Who should be contacted – family, friends, colleagues at work?

What would you like on the headstone?

Other

Will the surviving spouse know what electrician, plumber or other service technician to use?

The answers may be as simple as 'I don't care,' or much more complex. Whatever the answer, at least your survivors will be more easily able to plan what happens next, no matter what has happened to you.

The funeral arrangements may sound gruesome, but my mother had all that written down, and it was an incredible help at a difficult and emotional time. She was extremely thoughtful and considerate of others and wanted to make things as easy for her children as possible. I believe that once she had all of her plans in place, she relaxed considerably knowing she had done all she could. Planning ahead for death is a tremendous act of generosity and thoughtfulness.

There are no doubt other considerations A please add your own or modify these to suit your life's situation and plan.

Now ask, if it isn't you that dies or has a serious illness, do you know the answers to the above questions for your spouse, your children, your parents? It may not be easy to get the answers to these concerns from any of the aforementioned people, but your leading the way should help.

There are any number of approaches depending on the personality of the individual. The most direct, obviously, is to ask the questions above plus any others you deem appropriate. Some people are uncomfortable talking about these kinds of things at any age, and some may become more uncomfortable as they reach an age where it is more likely that they will die.

I think that if there is resistance, the single best approach is to talk about what you have done in this regard, explaining that you have talked with your spouse and made a list of your accounts because you want it to be as easy and uncomplicated for all who are remaining.

Failing that, if you speak with them about their past, as mentioned in Chapter 3, ease the questions into the present and gently probe in the areas listed above. This approach can also be taken when talking casually about present day events. For example, when the death of someone is in the news, you can again try talking about your preferences for cremation or burial, pallbearers, type of service and so forth, and ask about theirs. You may not get all the questions answered, but some of them surely will be.

Planning for Yourself
"If you don't know where you're going, any road will take you there." This is a way to live life. It is a way, however, that opens you up to missed opportunities and regrets as your life progresses. Part of the comfort of conscious living is knowing what you want to do with your life. You will have direction rather than wandering aimlessly. Also, if you determine your beliefs in what will happen to you after death, in God or not, or any other spiritual aspect that is of interest or concern, though you will not know with a one hundred per cent certainty what will happen until it does, it can set aside this important aspect of your life and

allow you to focus on the rest.

As you are planning your future, and reviewing your past to learn from it, beware of the "If onlys." These are two of the most damaging words in the English language.

"If only... I won the lottery... (Possible, not likely)

"If only... I'd spent twenty years studying in a Tibetan monastery with monks..." (Chances

are you didn't.)

"If only... I was an indigenous shaman..." (Chances are you aren't.)

"If only... I was a rich and famous movie star..." (You get the point.)

How much time do you spend with "If onlys?"

How much do we let "If onlys" affect our lives and self-esteem?

If it's something you really want, plan for it in the present and make it happen. But, be realistic about your expectations, otherwise you set yourself up for failure.

Having this plan and direction will at least allow you to live your life in a positive way and reduce the likelihood of regrets. True, you may not achieve every goal you set for yourself, and your direction may change, but at least you know what you are trying to achieve and will certainly find some goodness and happiness along the way.

In order to adequately plan for the future, we need to have some idea of where we want to go. In constructing this plan, there are a number of factors to keep in mind:

- Be realistic. You may have been told you can be anything you want to be – so you've set your sights on being the Queen of England, or the Dalai Lama. You are not likely to be either.

- Know that change will happen. No matter how good your plan is, changes will occur. Flexibility in your approach to this plan is important.

- Be aware of the physical needs of life on earth – money for living expenses, food, housing, and so on.
- The considerations listed below contain no right or wrong. What makes sense to you and what you want to do will likely be different from the next person, and that's okay.

Think about your life. Are there factors other than the above that should be considered when making your plan? Add them to the list.

Some of the areas that you should consider as you plan your conscious life are:

- What kind of work would you like to do, and can you earn a living doing it?
- If you don't think you can reasonably earn a living doing what your truly love, what can you do that will allow you to earn a living and give you time to do what you really want to do?
- Do you want to devote all or part of your life to helping others, financially or on a volunteer basis?
- What would you like your overall financial situation to be?
- What kind of home would you like to have and where should it be located?
- What kind of social life would you like?
- Do you want to be married or single? Would you like to have children?
- Do you want to travel?
- Do you have a bucket list of things that you want to do?
- What are the spiritual aspects of your life?
- What do you want to do when you retire?
- I don't believe that retirement should be the focus of your life or that your whole life plan should be designed for your retirement. However, it is part of your life and as you

age, it will become more important. And, as you construct your life plan and think about what you might like to do in retirement, you can factor that into your plan. For example, if painting is an interest, but perhaps not your primary interest in life, you can include in your plan: time to paint, lessons, trips to art museums, books on painting and whatever else comes to mind.

There may very well be other aspects you would like to examine. By all means, add to or modify any questions above to fit your particular situation.

Now, in order to define how you want to live and what you would like to do with your life, try this meditation – consider in this the results of the Meditation for Aging:

Meditation to Live Consciously

Sit or lie in a comfortable position.

Take several comfortable breaths, the more the better.

Focus on each in-breath.

Then, focus on each out-breath.

Now, on each in-breath, breathe in positive energy and relaxation.

On each out-breath, allow all tension, stress and negative thoughts to leave your body.

Continue until you are totally relaxed.

After you are relaxed, feel a cool breeze flow through your mind taking away all thoughts and concerns.

Let it keep flowing until your mind is clear.

Now, imagine that it is five years from today and you are sitting in a comfortable chair reading your favorite newspaper.

On the front page you see an article about you and your accomplishments. It includes your job, personal interests, plans for retirement, aging, financial situation, where you live, a bit about your married life, your social life, your spiritual beliefs and other pertinent information.

Take some time and read it.

What does it say?

Is this what you want it to say?

Is it reporting the accomplishments you had hoped for?

Are you doing the work you wanted to do?

If not, take a few moments and decide what you would like it to say.

Take as much time as you need to rewrite the article.

Take several breaths and relax even deeper.

Now, envision what you need to do to make this happen?

Take a few moments to consider the actions you need to take.

Resolve to do it.

Take a few more comfortable breaths as you enjoy the feeling of accomplishment for living the life you want in a conscious way, and the peace and harmony it brings you.

Here's a shortcut to help you remember:

Breathe

Relax

Clear mind

Define your plan

Visualize yourself enjoying your new life plan

Breathe.

I would suggest that after doing this meditation the first time, take notes and allow a couple of days to pass. Review your notes and do the meditation again. The purpose of subsequent meditations is to fill in any areas that may not have been covered the first time and to review the path you have selected. It may very well be that in each meditation part of your life's plan will manifest, and it could take two or three (or more) for the full plan to develop. This is okay and normal – whatever works best for you is the right way. You may, in fact, wish to deliberately focus on one or more topics each time. Again, do what is best for you.

When should you begin to plan ahead? Now! Why wait? If you're thirty or sixty, do the meditation above and start planning. Be ready to help create your future. Looking ahead at any point allows you to consider different options in all aspects of your planning.

Now you have an idea of how you can live consciously and have established a plan to get you there, to work towards what you want. And, don't be harsh on yourself if you get off track from time to time. Just remember, whatever you do, do it because you like to, do the best you can – whether you win the PGA or not isn't important, that you like to play golf and you play to the best of your ability, is.

You may realize at some point that you're not going to be able to do everything you want to, or even that one thing that you'd always hoped to do – such as, as Marianne Faithful sings, "Drive through Paris with the wind in your hair." Why not plan now to do the realistic things that you want. This doesn't mean that you have to quit work; as I mentioned earlier, there is the support side of your life that can't be ignored, but is sometimes merely a challenge to be overcome.

To execute your plan, try to be more present, more aware of what you're doing – appreciate every day and each person in your life – don't expect everyone to be perfect.

To keep yourself on track, remind yourself periodically of what your plan is. If you take your notes from your meditation(s), organize them by subject, keeping dates in mind if appropriate. You may want to write yourself a sticky note as a reminder of a particular goal, or create affirmations for yourself to keep you focused and on track.

Affirmations give you focus to do what you want to do, and

can help increase your confidence to do so. They are always stated in a positive way, and they are constructed as though their message has already happened. They are stated in the present, not the future.

For example, if your interest is painting, your affirmation would not be, "I'm going to become a painter." You would say, write and think, "I am a painter." This is a positive statement and says that you are a painter now, not in some unspecified future.

Try it. Use an interest that you are either just beginning or will begin in the near future. Say, "I am a(n) _____(fill in the blank)." You will be amazed at how different, good, and confident you feel.

Affirmations can be specific or they can be general. One of my favorites is from the five principles of Reiki. "Just for today, I will be kind to every living thing."

One last point I'd like to make is that we need to recognize, as my wife once said about knitting, "When you're knitting, you knit one stitch at a time." So, if you're knitting a sweater, or trying to achieve the goal(s) in your life plan, take one step at a time, and be mindful of that step.

We've talked a lot about doing, but sometimes it is best to give yourself permission not to do something, it can reduce stress and pressure and can also be part of your plan. As a reward for all your work, take a relaxing walk or bath or swim, or whatever is appealing to you and just enjoy your surroundings. Think of nothing but where you are – and relax.

9

Start Living Now!

O monks, just like examining gold in order to know its quality,
You should put my words to the test.
A wise person does not accept them merely out of respect.
– The Buddha (from *For the Benefit of All Beings* by
the Dalai Lama)

The above quote is similar in many ways to the quote at the beginning of Chapter 6, but it is important advice. Essentially what the Buddha is saying, is that no matter what you have read – this book or any other book, no matter what CD or DVD or workshop has provided information to you, consider it, think about it, and examine it in terms of your current knowledge and beliefs. Ask yourself, "How does it feel? Does it make sense to you? Is it advice/knowledge that you can use and integrate into your spiritual tapestry?"

If it doesn't fit directly, ask if some modification makes more sense. Always keep in mind that whoever has provided this advice has not lived your life – has not experienced life and its happiness or pain or sorrow as you have. As the Buddha has said, make sure that whatever you integrate into your way of life, do it because it makes sense to you.

As a direct result of my near-death experience, I still, whenever I hear on the radio or television or read in the paper about someone dying, whether from illness, accident or foul play, it serves as another reminder of how fortunate I've been and the gratitude I feel for everything and everyone around me. I also occasionally pause to consider what people may think about me after I die. This may sound morbid, but I assure you it's not. It is, in many ways, like affirmations, 'I am thankful I am alive and for all that is a part of my life,' or 'I live consciously and accomplish my goals.'

One of the key points I hope you take from this book and my experience is that while we usually don't plan to die, it still happens, and can at any time, whether by accident, illness or other methods. This in itself is good motivation to live consciously.

In addition to death, we have examined another key part of life – aging. We've explored ways to incorporate aging and death into a conscious life, a life that is directed, and a life that may very well change. The reality is that you may not fulfill every aspect of your dream, your planned life, but even if you don't reach it, trying can be fun and rewarding. For example, let's say that one of your goals is to visit all the locations in the book *1000 Places To See Before You Die* by Patricia Schulz. You may not get to them all, but there can be much enjoyment in the attempt. You don't have to look back and wonder what it might have been like, you did as much as you reasonably could.

A further important aspect to keep in mind is that even though you have a great plan and are living the conscious life that you would like to, change does happen. You could become sick, or your spouse or your parents. You know this might happen and you might try to factor this into your plan. However, you can't know when or how serious the illness might be. If you can learn to accept change as part of your conscious life, it will make your life so much easier. It may be necessary to do the Meditation to Live Consciously in Chapter 8 again. Do it.

To help emphasize that we have made a transition from a non-directed to directed life, it is a good idea to acknowledge this transition in a formal way. There are any number of methods to accomplish this, but I'd like to talk about three of them.

The snake is a powerful shamanic symbol. To Native Americans, it is a symbol of transformation. A physical manifestation of this change is the shedding of its skin. It represents the old being discarded in favor of the new or the death of the old and the birth of the new.

A meditation on the snake shedding its skin represents leaving the old you, the old plan (or no plan) behind, and embarking on a new plan. This can be used to emphasize and reinforce any kind of change you want to use it for, including habits, jobs, relationships or other. If you would like to use a visualization of this kind of change in your meditation, simply replace the lines below between the dashes and substitute them with a vision of you, as the snake shedding its skin - your past plan - and emerging as the new person to follow your new conscious life.

Another way to shed unwanted parts of the past is the Mayan Fire Ceremony. This too, is a good way to shed old habits, relationships, attitudes and so on. In its purest form, you would go into nature and gather sticks, leaves or other natural items, and make a figure out of the items. Meditate or simply relax in nature or a quiet place in your home, and imbue the figure with whatever habit, thought, way of life, relationship or other situation you want to change in your life. Acknowledge that you are consciously making a change, then, place it in a fire, bury it, or cast it in a stream and watch it float away. You can use just sticks or leaves or if you're in the city, a letter, picture or any article, really, to represent that which you want to remove from your life, and as you burn or discard it by whatever method, feel and/or visualize yourself casting the old part of your life away and move to the new way of being.

The keys here, are:

Obtain/create a representational item - from nature if possible.

Project or visualize into the object that part of your life - no matter what it is, a problem, concept, relationship, habit,

or in our case now, an old or no direction in life - that you
want to leave behind.

Just before disposing of it, say a few words to consciously
acknowledge that you are making a break with the past
and are looking forward to a new future.

Dispose of it.

The last method I'd like to discuss is the subject of the Meditation
to Shed the Past – crossing a bridge. The symbolism here is
probably quite obvious – the old part of your life, the part you
want to change, whatever that happens to be, is on one side of the
bridge – the new part of your life is on the other side. You leave
the old and go on to the new. As you cross the bridge,
acknowledge the change you are making, out loud or silently.

Whichever method you choose, the important components
are the same:

• Consciously acknowledge that there is a part of your life
  or the direction you want your life to take, that you want
  to change;
• Select a method to do this;
• Do it;
• Commit to the change.

Meditation to Shed the Past

Sit or lie in a comfortable position.

Take several comfortable breaths, the more the better.

Focus on each in-breath.

Then, focus on each out-breath.

Now, on each in-breath, breathe in positive energy and
relaxation.

On each out-breath, allow all tension, stress and negative
thoughts to leave your body.

Continue until you are totally relaxed.

After you are relaxed, feel a cool breeze flow through your
mind taking away all thoughts and concerns.
Let it keep flowing until your mind is clear.

Picture yourself standing at the side of a stream.
There is some grass, a few bushes and a few trees.
The grass is turning brown and many leaves have fallen from
the trees.
You look across the bridge and see lush green grasses,
flowers, bushes and trees.
You know you are in the right place at the right time.
The temperature is just the way you like it – feel it.
You, the old you, the you before you planned your conscious
life, stands there, looking across the bridge.
You pause, momentarily recalling the way you had lived
your life before your meditations and decision to live
consciously and how you wanted to do it.
You take the first steps, thinking about the old way.
You may feel a slight shiver of fear – you are moving into the
unknown.
That is only momentary.
A strength surges through you – a confidence – a knowing
that you are doing what needs to be done -a knowing that
your life will be more directed and rewarding.
You pause now, in the middle of the bridge, and say goodbye
to what you are leaving behind – this may again be out
loud or silently.
After a moment, you stride forward confidently, crossing the
rest of the bridge, entering your new life.

Take a few more comfortable breaths as you enjoy the new
you embarking on a new directed plan for your conscious
life.
Sit or lie for as long as you would like, feeling your new life

emerging.

When you're ready, open your eyes, and come back to the new here and now.

Here's a shortcut to help you remember:
Breathe
Relax
Clear mind
Visualize the old you becoming the new you as you cross the
    bridge
Enjoy.
Breathe.

As I've mentioned before, you may want to record the above meditation (as well as any of the others) or have a friend read it to you so that you can truly relax into it without the distraction of reading it. Either way is okay.

You have now created direction in your life – perhaps new, perhaps confirming that what you have been doing is what you should be doing and what you want to do. You have crossed the bridge to your new life. You have committed to this direction, to living consciously. As we've recognized, this path will not always be the way we envision and want it to be. There will be challenges along the way, which, after all, makes life interesting.

To minimize stress that we may encounter as we live through our planned direction, I would like to offer a few very simple meditations. These can be done at home, at work or most anywhere except driving, operating machinery, or any other task which requires your full attention.

One of my favorite expressions is: "Don't just do something, sit there." I don't know who originally said it, but it is sometimes the best solution. We push ourselves, to do this or accomplish that, or for one reason or another, come under stress at work or at home. Often, we can do more to help ourselves spiritually, emotionally and physically by just chilling out, relaxing – by just sitting there, with no focus or thoughts. We can calm our minds and hearts, lower our blood pressure and then interact with others more effectively.

The next one is simple, it is pure, it is more powerful that you can imagine. No matter how you choose to live your life consciously, do this meditation daily, or as often as you can. It is something you can do for you, and could help you no matter what is going on in your life. I feel more relaxed just thinking about it.

I call it the Meditation Simple, though it really doesn't need a name. The introductory words will sound familiar. They are at the beginning of all of the meditations in this book. Meditations can be very complex or very simple – I prefer simple.

I suggest focusing on your breath, though you could repeat a mantra, affirmation or any words of your choosing, focus on the emptiness of space, or use repetitive drumming or rattles. The point is to allow your mind to be empty of all thoughts and allow you to go into the emptiness, to escape your ego, to feel the pureness of you. If thoughts do intrude, acknowledge them and let them go. If you can do this for ten to fifteen minutes a day, you will be more relaxed and able to deal with challenging issues in a less stressful way. And, by clearing out your mind periodically, who knows what wonderful, creative or spiritual thoughts may be stimulated?

Meditation Simple

Sit or lie in a comfortable position.

Take several comfortable breaths, the more the better.

Focus on each in-breath.

Then, focus on each out-breath.

Now, on each in-breath, breathe in positive energy and relaxation.

On each out-breath, allow all tension, stress and negative

thoughts to leave your body.

Keep your mind clear.

View it as a white board and erase any thoughts that come in.

Or, view it as the emptiness in space, or, simply acknowledge any thoughts that come in and let them pass through.

Continue as long as you can (15 seconds to 15 minutes).

Continue until you are totally relaxed.

Slowly bring yourself back to conscious awareness.

You will be surprised at how relaxed you will feel and the clarity of mind you have after you have completed this brief meditation.

One final suggested meditation is even simpler:

Stand in a relaxed position,

Empty your mind,

Just breathe for thirty seconds, or ten minutes, whatever is appropriate for you.

This is great for taking a mini-break at work.

The Buddha advises us to think for ourselves. I have offered some thoughts and suggestions to you about how to live life, but remember, no matter who says what, a religious leader, a political leader, friends, family, or even me, we all come from our own experiences, have our own thoughts, ideas and ways of living that make sense to us. You have your own. If my suggestions make sense to you, use them or modify them or develop your own. In living a positive, loving and compassionate life filled with appreciation and gratitude, no matter how your path develops, these attitudes will be helpful in how you approach life and death and challenges you encounter.

An old Chinese proverb (at least it was in an old Chinese fortune cookie) says "Your happiness is before you, not behind you! Cherish it."

Remember, life may not be a fairy tale, but it can be meaningful, rewarding, interesting and fun – this is the promise of *Conscious Living Made Easy.*

Bibliography

Easwaran, Eknath. *The Bhagavad Gita.* Petaluma, California: Nilgiri Press, 1985.

Easwaran, Eknath. *The Dhammapada.* Petaluma, California: Nilgiri Press, 1986.

Hanh, Thich Nhat. *The Miracle of Mindfulness.* Boston: Beacon Press, 1987.

Hanh, Thich Nhat. *Peace Is Every Step.* New York: Bantam Books, 1991.

Johnson, Spencer. *The Present.* New York: Doubleday, 2003.

Perkins, John. *The World Is As You Dream It.* Rochester, Vermont: Destiny Books, 1994.

Perkins, John. *Shapeshifting.* Rochester, Vermont: Destiny Books, 1997.

Roberts, Llyn. *The Good Remembering.* Winchester, U.K., New York: O-Books, 2007.

Roberts, Llyn and Levy, Robert. *Shamanic Reiki.* Winchester, U.K., New York: O-Books, 2007.

Schulz, Patricia, *1000 Places to See Before You Die: A Traveler's Life List.* New York: Workman Publishing Company, 2003.

Shimoff, Marci and Kline, Carol. *Happy for No Reason: 7 Steps to Being Happy from the Inside Out.* New York: Free Press, 2009.

Southard, Robert Y. *Ordinary Secrets: Notes for Your Spiritual Journey.* Winchester, U.K., New York: O-Books, 2007.

About the Author

Bob Southard is a businessman with a B.S. in Psychology and an M.B.A. He is a Certified Hypnotherapist, Shamanic Reiki Master Practitioner and Usui Shiki Ryoho Reiki Master, and has worked with a number of shamans in the United States, the highlands of Ecuador and the Amazon for many years. Bob currently sits on the Dream Change board of directors.

He also developed the HypnoJourney™, a combination of ancient and traditional shamanic journeying practices with more modern hypnosis techniques, after more than fifteen years of study and practice in shamanic journeying and hypnosis. He offers workshops featuring the HypnoJourney™ process and produces HypnoJourney™ CDs so others can benefit from this practice on their own.

He lives in eastern Massachusetts in the U.S. For more information about Bob and his work and to learn about Dream Change:

www.bostonmystery.com and www.dreamchange.org

BOOKS

O is a symbol of the world, of oneness and unity. In different cultures it also means the "eye," symbolizing knowledge and insight. We aim to publish books that are accessible, constructive and that challenge accepted opinion, both that of academia and the "moral majority."

Our books are available in all good English language bookstores worldwide. If you don't see the book on the shelves ask the bookstore to order it for you, quoting the ISBN number and title. Alternatively you can order online (all major online retail sites carry our titles) or contact the distributor in the relevant country, listed on the copyright page.

See our website **www.o-books.net** for a full list of over 500 titles, growing by 100 a year.

And tune in to myspiritradio.com for our book review radio show, hosted by June-Elleni Laine, where you can listen to the authors discussing their books.

MySpiritRadio